S0-DXM-771

SHAWN MENDES

Tammy
Gagne

Mitchell Lane

PUBLISHERS
2001 SW 31st Avenue
Hallandale, FL 33009
www.mitchelllane.com

Mitchell Lane
PUBLISHERS

Copyright © 2019 by Mitchell Lane Publishers, Inc. All rights reserved. No part of this book may be reproduced without written permission from the publisher. Printed and bound in the United States of America.

Printing   1   2   3   4   5   6   7   8   9

A Robbie Reader Biography

Library of Congress Cataloging-in-Publication Data
Names: Gagne, Tammy, author.
Title: Shawn Mendes / by Tammy Gagne.
Description: Hallandale, FL : Mitchell Lane Publishers, [2019] | Series: A Robbie reader | Includes bibliographical references and index.
Identifiers: LCCN 2018008729 | ISBN 9781680201949 (library bound)
Subjects: LCSH: Mendes, Shawn, 1998- —Juvenile literature | Singers—Canada—Biography—Juvenile literature.
Classification: LCC ML3930.M444 G34 2018 | DDC 782.42164092 [B] —dc23
LC record available at https://lccn.loc.gov/2018008729

eBook ISBN: 978-1-68020-195-6

ABOUT THE AUTHOR: Tammy Gagne has written more than 200 books for both adults and children. Her titles include numerous books about musicians—including *Charlie Puth* and *Ed Sheeran*. She resides in northern New England with her husband and son.

PUBLISHER'S NOTE: The following story has been thoroughly researched and to the best of our knowledge represents a true story. While every possible effort has been made to ensure accuracy, the publisher will not assume liability for damages caused by inaccuracies in the data, and makes no warranty on the accuracy of the information contained herein. This story has not been authorized or endorsed by Shawn Mendes.

CONTENTS

Words in bold type can be found in the glossary.

Shawn Mendes rose to fame by posting videos to the Vine app. Now he performs all over the world. He is seen here at Spotify's Inaugural Secret Genius Awards in Los Angeles in 2017.

1 A VERY HAPPY BIRTHDAY

"Is there anything you want?" Annabelle asked her big brother as she flipped through a music magazine. Colby's birthday was in just a few days, and she still hadn't found the perfect gift.

"You don't have to buy me anything," he told her. It sounded like something their parents would say—until he added, "You can just stay out of my room for the next year."

She stuck her tongue out at him as she rolled her eyes, otherwise ignoring the comment. But she also smiled. They had always gotten along this way. They pretended to drive each other crazy. But

> **Colby's birthday was in just a few days, and she still hadn't found the perfect gift.**

5

born exactly one year and two days apart, they were actually each other's best friend. Many people even thought they were twins.

"Hey," she asked him, "did you see that Taylor Swift **serenaded** Shawn Mendes on his birthday? She got the whole audience at one of her concerts to sing 'Happy Birthday' to him?" She knew that Taylor Swift was Colby's favorite singer.

Taylor
Swift

"Okay, get me that instead," he added. "I want to be serenaded by Taylor Swift."

"In your dreams!" Annabelle teased as she skimmed the concert dates at the bottom of the page. "Speaking of Taylor Swift and Shawn Mendes," she said, "they will be performing here in just a few weeks. I wonder if there are any tickets left." Shawn Mendes was Annabelle's favorite.

"Let's check," Colby suggested as he picked up his smartphone to search for info on the show. "It could be our birthday presents to each other."

"That's not a bad idea," Annabelle agreed. "I'm surprised you thought of it." This time it was Colby's turn to roll his eyes.

In the last few years, Shawn Mendes has become one of the

> In the last few years, Shawn Mendes has become one of the most popular musicians in the world. It all started with an app called Vine.

most popular musicians in the world. It all started with an app called Vine. Back in 2013, Shawn used the social media platform to post videos of himself singing. His future manager, Andrew Gertler, discovered his commanding voice on a cover of A Great Big World's "Say Something." Even though

Shawn had never sold a song, Gertler thought the teen had what it took to make it in the music business. Just two years later the young musician was opening for Taylor Swift.

Shawn Mendes performs during Taylor Swift: The 1989 World Tour in Seattle on August 8, 2015.

2 MUSIC'S FIRST VINE STAR

Shawn Peter Raul Mendes was born on August 8, 1998, in Toronto, Ontario, Canada. He grew up in Pickering, a city east of Toronto. His mother, Karen, was a real estate agent. His father, Manuel, was a businessman who sold restaurant supplies. Even though neither one of them was musical, Shawn sees himself as following in their footsteps. He says that like them, he is an **entrepreneur** of sorts.

Shawn's younger sister, Aaliyah, also sings. She has more than 240,000 followers on her own Vine account. But she has not decided to pursue a musical career yet. Social media certainly helped Shawn make

Shawn's younger sister, Aaliyah, also sings.

a name for himself, though. Not only was he discovered online, but he also looked to the internet for musical instruction. He taught himself to play the guitar in 2012 by watching videos on YouTube.

One of the first songs he learned to play was Train's "Hey, Soul Sister." At that time he didn't even know the names of the chords he was playing. He has said that he wasn't very good at first. But he kept at it, practicing for hours each day. He also started posting his songs for anyone who cared to listen to them.

One of the first songs that Shawn posted was a cover of Bieber's song "As Long as You Love Me." The recording went viral.

At first he wasn't trying to do anything more than have fun. He enjoyed playing his music and sharing it with others. But then he realized social media presented a huge opportunity. In addition to posting his music, he began interacting with his growing number of

followers. He asked them what they would like to hear him sing. He then recorded those songs and posted them to Vine and YouTube.

Other stars, such as Justin Bieber, had been discovered through YouTube. But this was the first time a musician would use Vine in the same way. One of the first songs that Shawn posted was a cover of Bieber's song "As Long as You Love Me." The recording went **viral**.

3 KEEPING IT REAL

Shortly after Andrew Gertler heard Shawn sing, he flew the entire Mendes family to New York City. There, Gertler had Shawn record some music in a professional studio. He wanted to get a better feel for how much talent the young singer had. While it was raw, the talent was definitely there.

Shawn had a natural **flair** for performing. And he didn't just want to sing. He also wanted to write his own material. He had already written many songs by this time. He performed them for Gertler, who was again impressed. Shawn told him that he saw himself as a songwriter and wanted to record his own music.

> Shawn had a natural flair for performing. And he didn't just want to sing.

Andrew Gertler and Eric Wong from Island Records pose with Shawn Mendes at the company's 2015 holiday party in New York City.

CHAPTER 3

Life was about to change dramatically for the young artist. Back in Pickering, Shawn had been a regular student at Pine Ridge Secondary School. He enjoyed playing hockey and soccer. But he wasn't the most popular kid in school. In 2016, Gertler told *Rolling Stone*, "He always tells me that early on when he was starting to sing and starting to post covers–and this was before anything happened and before anything went viral–he would go to school and people would make fun of him." Luckily, he had a small group of good friends who were kinder. And his family always supported him.

> One of Shawn's idols was Ed Sheeran. Shawn liked how he put his talent on display without acting too flashy.

One of Shawn's idols was Ed Sheeran. Shawn liked how he put his talent on display without acting too flashy. He also admired that Sheeran wrote his own music. Since his own rise to stardom, Shawn has gotten to

Shawn and Ed Sheeran perform "Mercy" during the Illuminate tour on August 16, 2017, in New York City.

meet Sheeran. He found him to be exactly as he seemed. He thinks the singer's down-to-earth nature is the best thing about him.

Shawn isn't afraid to show his fans his own easygoing nature. When performing a concert, Shawn is known to ask for the lights to be turned up at certain moments. This allows him to see the faces of the people who come to see him play. He likes knowing that, instead of just a featureless crowd, they are real people, much like him.

STRAIGHT TO NUMBER ONE

Shawn signed with Island Records in 2014. In July of that year, he released his **debut** extended-play record, or EP. This format allows artists to release more than just a single without having to record a standard-length album. *The Shawn Mendes EP* had four songs. It hit number one on iTunes in just 37 minutes. In October, *Time* magazine named Shawn one of its 25 Most Influential Teens of 2014.

At just 16, Shawn was traveling the world as he began promoting

The *Shawn Mendes EP* had four songs. It hit number one on iTunes in just **37** minutes.

Shawn visited the Sirius XM Studios on July 22, 2014.

his music on a wider level. Still technically enrolled at Pine Ridge, he was now taking online classes as he moved through his junior year. He has shared that the music industry has caused him to grow up more quickly than he would have as a typical teen back home in Pickering. Perhaps it is that **maturity** that has inspired some of his new goals. For example, he has said that he doesn't want to be just a teen idol.

> For a long time, Shawn didn't think he deserved all the attention he was getting. Even now, he has said he feels great pressure to live up to people's expectations.

He wants parents to know his music–and enjoy it–as well.

He doesn't see his youth as something that limits him in any way. Still, he remains **humble**. For a long time, Shawn didn't think he deserved all the attention he was getting. Even now, he has said he feels great pressure to live up to people's expectations.

Shawn is seen here performing at Radio Disney's Family VIP Birthday on November 22, 2014 at Club Nokia in Los Angeles.

John Mayer

That part of fame has been stressful for him. He copes by putting as much time and effort into his art as he can. Gertler said Shawn is rarely seen without a guitar in his hand. He still practices as much, if not more, than he did back when he was still learning the instrument.

Another one of Shawn's idols is John Mayer. The singer-songwriter sent Shawn a guitar in 2016. Shawn told *Rolling Stone* that they began talking afterwards and hoped to find some time to work together down the road. In April 2017, Mayer surprised his own fans in Toronto by bringing Shawn out on stage during his Search for Everything world tour. They performed Shawn's hit "Mercy" and Mayer's song "In Your Atmosphere."

5 NOTHING HOLDING HIM BACK

Shawn released his first full-length album, *Handwritten*, in 2015. Just a little more than a year later, he told *Rolling Stone* that some of the songs made him **cringe**. "I'm just growing so quickly, so my songs are quickly changing on me. But it's fine. I love them for what they are, and what they were, to me."

SHAWN MENDES
HANDWRITTEN

He released his second LP, *Illuminate*, in 2016. He has said that John Mayer was a big influence on him when he was writing

He released his second LP, *Illuminate*, in 2016.

21

The first show in Shawn's Illuminate tour brought him to the Hydro arena in Glasgow, Scotland.

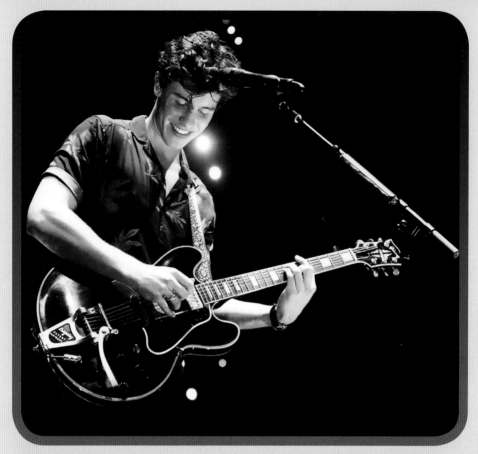

Shawn's joy in performing comes through loud and clear when he is on stage. He is seen here playing at the ORACLE Arena in Oakland, California.

the songs. He is still amazed by the fact that they have become such good friends.

Shawn has racked up his share of awards since arriving on the music scene. In 2015, he won a Teen Choice Award for Choice Webstar: Music. In 2016, he earned a Kids' Choice Award for Favorite New Artist. Like Shawn himself, the honors seem to be growing up. In 2017, he won an American Music Award for Favorite Adult Contemporary Artist.

Shawn won the American Music Award for Favorite Adult Contemporary Artist in 2017.

When Shawn isn't accepting awards or performing, he still spends time in Pickering with his family. He calls the city the most comforting place in the world. He tries hard not to think about his fame too much. He thinks that is a mistake that many performers make. Instead, he just tries to have fun and work at what he loves.

Shawn made some time to take selfies with some of his London fans at the SSE Arena, Wembley in 2017.

Shawn now has more than 29 million followers on Instagram and about 18 million followers on Twitter. He has learned that this large audience can help him accomplish more than just selling records. When Mexico was hit with a devastating earthquake in 2017, Shawn joined forces with

Gertler is as impressed with Shawn as a person as he is by his musical talent.

the Red Cross to help raise money for the survivors. After donating $100,000 to the cause along with his management company, he posted a video asking his fans to help out, too.

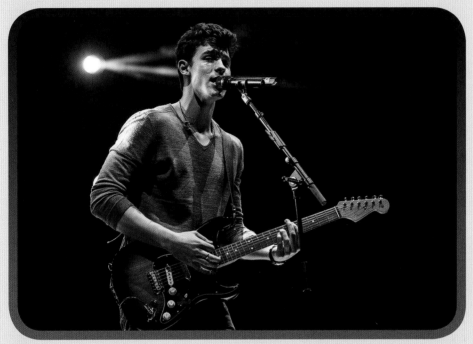

Shawn enjoys using his talent to help others, as he did at the Rays of Sunshine charity concert in London.

Gertler is as impressed with Shawn as a person as he is by his musical talent. In an interview with *Rolling Stone*, he pointed out that despite Shawn's success, who he is hasn't changed. "He does a good job of surrounding himself with great people and also of keeping himself in the right mindset."

CHRONOLOGY

1998 Shawn Mendes is born on August 8.

2012 Shawn begins teaching himself to play the guitar from watching YouTube videos.

2013 Andrew Gertler discovers Shawn on Vine.

2014 Shawn signs with Island Records. His debut EP hits number one on iTunes in just 37 minutes.

2015 Shawn tours as an opening act for Taylor Swift. Shawn wins the Teen Choice Award for Choice Webstar: Music.

2016 He wins the Kids' Choice Award for Favorite New Artist.

2017 Shawn joins John Mayer on stage at a concert in Toronto. He wins the American Music Award for Favorite Adult Contemporary Artist.

DISCOGRAPHY

2014 *The Shawn Mendes EP*
2015 *Handwritten*
2016 *Illuminate*

FIND OUT MORE

Shawn Mendes: Superstar Next Door. Chicago: Triumph
    Books, 2016.
Croft, Malcolm. *Shawn Mendes: Ultimate Fan Book*.
    London: Carlton Books, 2017.
Ed Sheeran. Official website.
    http://www.edsheeran.com/?frontpage=true
John Mayer. Official website.
    http://johnmayer.com/
Shawn Mendes. Official website.
    http://www.shawnmendesofficial.com/
Taylor Swift. Official website.
    https://www.taylorswift.com/
Zakarin, Debra Mostow. *Shawn Mendes: It's My Time*.
    New York: Scholastic, 2016.

WORKS CONSULTED

Ceron, Ella. "Shawn Mendes's First Vine Isn't What You'd
    Expect." *Teen Vogue*, October 27, 2016. https://www.
    teenvogue.com/story/shawn-mendes-first-vine

Harper, Simon. "Glow Your Own Way: Shawn Mendes
    Interviewed." *Clash*, June 9, 2017. http://www.
    clashmusic.com/features/glow-your-own-way-
    shawn-mendes-interviewed

Ranscombe, Sian. "Shawn Mendes: How a six-second
    video launched the next Justin Bieber." *The Telegraph*,
    January 16, 2015. http://www.telegraph.co.uk/
    culture/music/11340960/Shawn-Mendes-How-a-
    six-second-video-launched-the-next-Justin-Bieber.
    html

WORKS CONSULTED

"Shawn Mendes: Biography." IMDB. http://www.imdb.
com/name/nm6658398/bio

"Shawn Mendes On Leap From Vine Star to Major Label
Target: 'It was absolutely insane.'" *Billboard*, July 23,
2014. http://www.billboard.com/articles/columns/
pop-shop/6176073/shawn-mendes-on-leap-from-
vine-star-to-major-label-target-it-was

Spanos, Brittany. "Shawn Mendes: How a Toronto
Teen Became the Superstar Next Door." *Rolling Stone*,
April 13, 2016. http://www.rollingstone.com/music/
features/shawn-mendes-how-a-toronto-teen-
became-the-superstar-next-door-20160413

Tanzer, Myles. "Shawn Mendes On How To Write A
Love Song And Stay Away From The Internet." *Fader*,
July 26, 2016. http://www.thefader.
com/2016/07/26/shawn-mendes-interview-
illuminate

Tenreyro, Tatiana. "Shawn Mendes Teams Up With Red
Cross For Mexico Earthquake Relief Campaign,
$100,000 Already Donated." *Billboard*, September
22, 2017. https://www.billboard.com/articles/
columns/pop/7973742/shawn-mendes-red-cross-
mexico-earthquake-donated

Weatherby, Taylor. "John Mayer & Shawn Mendes Duet
on Mash-Up on 'Mercy' and 'In Your Atmosphere' in
Toronto." *Billboard*, April 4, 2017. https://www.
billboard.com/articles/columns/pop/7751409/john-
mayer-shawn-mendes-duet-mash-up-mercy-in-
your-atmosphere-video

GLOSSARY

cringe (KRINJ)–to react in distaste

debut (dey-BYOO)–a person's first appearance or performance in a particular capacity or role

entrepreneur (ahn-truh-pruh-NUR)–a person who manages a business or other large project

flair (FLAIR)–a natural talent or ability

humble (HUHM-buhl)–not arrogant

maturity (muh-CHOOR-i-tee)–state of being full grown

serenade (ser-uh-NEYD)–to entertain a person by singing to him or her

viral (VAYH-ruhl)–becoming extremely popular by circulating unusually quickly

PHOTO CREDITS: Cover, pp. 1, 3, 4–Frazer Harrison/Staff/Getty Images; p. 6–jazills/cc-by-sa 2.0; p. 8–Suzi Pratt/LP5/Contributor/Getty Images; pp. 11, 19–Disney Channel/Image Group LA/cc-by-nd 2.0; p. 13–Monica Schipper/Stringer/Getty Images; p. 15–Taylor Hill/Contributor/Getty Images; p. 17–Astrid Stawiarz/Contributor/Getty Images; p. 20–Gary Gershoff/Contributor/Getty Images; pp. 22-23–Roberto Ricciuti/Contributor/Getty Images; p. 24–Josiah VanDien/cc-by-sa 4.0; p. 25–Kevin Winter/Staff/Getty Images; p. 26–Jeff Kravitz/Contributor/Getty Images; p. 27–Neil Lupin/Contributor/Getty Images. Artwork: Freepiks.

INDEX